Outdoor Adventure Awaits

A Guide to Starting a Profitable Adventure Tourism Business

Table of Contents

Chapter 1. Introduction

As the burgeoning siren call of untamed wilderness beckons to more people than ever before, the thirst for outdoor adventure is rapidly growing into a profitable marketplace. Our Special Report, "Outdoor Adventure Awaits: A Guide to Starting a Profitable Adventure Tourism Business," will not only nourish your spirit of exploration but also equip you with the practical steps and knowledge to successfully ignite a prosperous business in this thrilling industry. Packed with in-depth research, expert opinions, and real-world case studies, our guide is the treasure map that future adventure tourism entrepreneurs didn't know they needed. Purchase this report now and embark on an expedition that takes you from passionate outdoor enthusiast to astute business owner, shaping memorable experiences and reaping financial rewards as your venture blossoms. Welcome to your exciting new venture, where the adventure truly never stops!

Chapter 2. Understanding the Landscape of Adventure Tourism

When you think of entering the exciting and lucrative world of adventure tourism, understanding the landscape of the industry is crucial. Let's immerse ourselves in this thrilling yet demanding terrain and unravel its many facets.

2.1. The Evolution of Adventure Tourism

Adventure tourism, an industry once relegated to the fringes of the tourism sector, has now assumed a place of prominence. In the past, this niche was interpreted strictly as high-risk activities for thrill-seekers. However, with changing times and evolving tourists' preferences, it's expanded its domain to include experiences focusing on nature, wildlife, and cultural explorations. The thrill factor, while still a driving force, now shares the stage with the quest for unique and genuine experiences.

Adventure tourism has emerged as an antidote to quantified, mechanized, and impersonal travel experiences. It provides tourists with the opportunity to explore offbeat paths, indulge in physical activities, and engage with local communities in meaningful ways. This transition reflects the trends of experiential and sustainable tourism, placing the industry in sync with the current global movements geared towards green, responsible living and travel.

2.2. The Market of Adventure Tourism

An understanding of the market in both its current form and future prospects is essential for aspiring entrepreneurs. As per the Adventure Travel Trade Association (ATTA), the global adventure tourism market was valued at approximately 683 billion dollars in 2017 and is projected to reach approximately 1.69 trillion dollars by 2026. A CAGR of around 10.26% during the forecast period sees to a profitable proposition.

The market is characterized by an increase in millennials and Gen Z travelers, who show an affinity towards experiences over material possessions. Adventure tourism caters perfectly to their need for self-discovery, self-expression, authentic experiences, and sustainability. Our report on 'The Quest for Experiences: A Millennial and Gen Z Perspective' further explores these evolving consumer preferences in the tourism sector.

Moreover, driven by social media exposure and emerging lifestyle trends, more people are seeking active and nature-based vacations. Thus, offering room for a myriad of adventure tourism offerings from hiking, trekking, wildlife safaris, to cultural tours, and eco-tours.

2.3. Length and Breadth of Services

Adventure tourism is an expansive field, opening up countless opportunities for budding entrepreneurs. To make an informed choice, you need to understand the full spectrum of services it encomasses.

At one end of the spectrum, we have 'Hard Adventures' which involve physically rigorous and high-risk activities, such as rock climbing, bungee jumping, mountaineering, and white-water rafting.

These activities demand technical expertise and stringent safety measures for both service providers and tourists.

Then, 'Soft Adventures' exist. They include less risky and physically demanding activities, such as hiking, cycling, bird-watching, or camping. These explorations engage you with natural or cultural landscapes and are particularly popular among family groups, seniors, and tourists looking for a gentle introduction to adventure tourism.

Moreover, there is an increasing demand for 'Educational Adventures'. They focus more on cultural exchange, local immersions, and imparting knowledge about natural heritage, climate change, conservation efforts, and more.

In addition, 'Luxury Adventure Travel,' with high-end, curated experiences that combine adventure with opulence, is emerging as a niche of significant potential, especially for high-income travelers seeking unique experiences.

2.4. Regulatory and Ethical Considerations

Every adventurous destination involves various social, environmental, and regulatory considerations. As an adventure tourism entrepreneur, you need to navigate these waters deliberately. The regulatory framework varies from country to country and often even within regions. As part of the due diligence, familiarize yourself with all local legislation, permits, and licenses needed to operate your business.

The environmental ethics of adventure tourism also bear immense significance. The industry thrives on unspoiled, pristine locations, demonstrating the close link between a healthy environment and a profitable adventure tourism business. Adopt sustainable practices and promote responsible tourism to safeguard the environment and ensure your business's longevity.

2.5. Partnering and Networking Opportunities

Collaboration is key in the adventure tourism business. The breadth and depth of services offered necessitate partnering with local communities, government bodies, tourism boards, and other businesses. These partnerships can offer significant infrastructural support, manpower, local expertise, and marketing benefits.

Building a network within the industry and related sectors can help you stay updated with current trends, regulatory changes, and opportunities for collaboration. Active participation in conventions, webinars, and industry associations such as the ATTA, can be beneficial in the long run.

Venturing into the adventure tourism business is bold and exciting. And this thorough understanding of the industry landscape will be your compass guiding through the thrilling terrain of opportunities. So, tighten your grip and prepare yourself for a rewarding entrepreneurial journey.

For more in-depth insights, case studies, and practical guides, explore other chapters of our comprehensive report, "Outdoor Adventure Awaits: A Guide to Starting a Profitable Adventure Tourism Business."

Purchase your copy today, and turn your passion for the outdoors into a thriving business venture!

Chapter 3. Scoping out Your Niche: Identifying Marketable Outdoor Activities

One of the first steps in starting a successful adventure tourism business is to identify a niche that suits your interests, experience, and market preferences. Finding this niche can prove to be a daunting endeavor, given the multitude of potential choices, but this selection process is crucial for your business's viability and longevity. Let's delve into the process of defining your niche in adventure tourism.

3.1. Understand the Adventure Tourism Landscape

Adventure tourism, at its very core, is about providing unique and riveting experiences in an outdoor setting. This could be anything from mountaineering to wildlife safaris, or scuba diving to bird-watching tours. Consequently, the first stage of your quest is to deeply understand the broad range of activities that fall under the umbrella of adventure tourism. Only when you have a clear picture of this variety will you be able to discern which of these activities could serve as potential niches for your business.

To understand the adventure tourism landscape, start with comprehensive market research. Look into well-established adventure tourism businesses, noting the activities they offer, the markets they target, and their unique selling points. Trade publications, industry reports, and international industry expos offer plenty of opportunity for insight.

Remember that while the industry is vast, consumer preferences can be fickle, and are often dictated by global and local trends. Keep an eye on the latest outdoor activity trends that people are talking about. Social media platforms, travel blogs, and adventure communities can provide useful insights into emerging trends.

3.2. Evaluate Your Skills, Interests, and Resources

Once you have a solid understanding of the breadth and depth of adventure tourism activities, your next step is to evaluate your own skills, interests, and available resources. What outdoor activity do you feel passionate about? Does it align with your skills and experiences? What resources are needed to transform your passion into a viable business? Do you have access to these resources or plans to acquire them?

For instance, if you are a seasoned hiker with a wealth of knowledge about local trails and topography, you might consider operating guided hiking tours. On the other hand, if you are an experienced surfer living near a coast, running a surfing school may better leverage your skills, experience, and location.

Beyond personal interests and skills, also consider logistical factors. For a successful venture, you need the right timing, location, and resources. If, say, you are passionate about skiing, does your locality feature ideal weather conditions and availability of slopes? Do you have or can you obtain the necessary permits, gear, and facilities?

3.3. Assess Market Demand

Having a passion and the means to start up a business is fantastic, but without demand, your venture might be short-lived. It is therefore critical to assess whether there is a market demand for the adventure activities you plan to offer.

Market demand can be determined through a series of methods such as surveys, focus groups, social listening, and secondary research on existing market data. When conducting market research, it's important to identify your target audience. Who are they? What are their preferences? How much are they willing to spend on outdoor activities?

Expanding upon the skiing example, does your town attract enough tourists during winter? Is there an existing market for ski lessons or guided ski tours, and if so, is it oversaturated? If you live in a metropolis, is there a white-collar crowd willing to pay for weekend skiing packages?

Also, consider broader trends. For example, the impact of climate change on season-bound activities like skiing and snowboarding should not be underestimated. With winters warming and snowfall becoming more unpredictable, the long-term viability of a winter sports-focused business needs to be evaluated carefully.

3.4. Fine-Tune Your Niche

The final step in the process is a combination of all the previous steps. Here, you further refine and specify your chosen niche. Do this by considering all the previous elements and developing a unique selling proposition (USP).

Your USP is what differentiates your business from competitors. It may be your location, expertise, type of activity, or charm of a personalized experience. Maybe you plan to offer unique, local routes that no other trekking company provides, or cater to a specialized market segment such as senior citizens or people with disabilities. The USP will help you zero in on a precise service that uses your strengths to meet demand and outshine competition. Carefully craft your brand around your USP, conveying to potential customers why your service is unique, desirable, and worth their while.

Remember, the best niches are not necessarily the most popular ones but those that you can serve exceptionally well. Being positioned in a smaller but underserved market segment where you can expertly deliver distinct value, often proves to be a sound strategic move that can lead to long-term profitability.

Identifying your marketable outdoor activity not only sets the direction of your adventure tourism venture but also acts as the catalyst to formulate your marketing strategies, hiring needs, investment planning, and more. Thus, make sure to invest time, research, and deliberate thought into this crucial business defining step.

Chapter 4. Preparing for the Journey: Business Plan Essentials

A solid business plan is integral to the establishment and operation of any successful enterprise, and adventure tourism is no exception. The necessity of a well-constructed business plan stems not just from the financial and logistical classification it provides, but also its communication abilities - it can effectively expose timely opportunities, underline hidden dangers, and vividly paint the prospects of your venture to investors, stakeholders, and potential partners.

4.1. Understanding the Tourism Market

Understanding the adventure tourism market is the first major step. Comprehensive knowledge of the market environment imparts an understanding of customer requirements, competitor insights, and market trends to gain an edge and remain relevant.

Firstly, identify your target audience by demographics, interests, and characteristics. Understand potential consumers' needs and offerings that will interest them. Consider conducting surveys or using online analytics tools for a precise assessment.

Secondly, recognize your strengths, weaknesses, opportunities, and threats (SWOT analysis). A SWOT analysis provides a clear perspective about your position in the market and helps identify opportunities you can seize and threats you need to be aware of.

Lastly, observe the competition. This would equip you with cues on what works and what doesn't, the pitfalls to avoid and successful practices to emulate.

4.2. Choosing your Niche

After understanding your market, it's important to choose your niche – specific adventures and experiences you want to center your business around. Choices can range from mountain climbing, kayaking, wildlife safaris, hiking, scuba diving, and more. This decision should be based on several factors such as personal interest, feasibility, and market potential. Further, carve your own unique selling points (USPs) within your choice of niche to differentiate yourself from competitors.

4.3. Legal Requirements

Adventure tourism businesses require adherence to multiple legal requirements from business registration, licensing, local council regulations, to specific activity licenses. Additionally, correct and comprehensive insurance coverage is paramount to buffer employee and customer risks. Make sure to research thoroughly on each of these aspects and comply with every requisite.

4.4. Financial Plan

Creating a realistic and detailed financial plan is an important aspect of your business plan. It should include your initial investment, projected income, estimated expenses, and break-even analysis.

The financial plan should also take into consideration unexpected costs and emergencies. This gives you, as well as potential investors, a clear picture of your financial requirements and the potential profitability of your venture.

4.5. Marketing and Promotion Strategy

Your marketing and promotional strategies should be based on your understanding of the target audience, market environment, and the specific experiences you are offering. These strategies can span over various channels such as social media platforms, digital advertising, specialized outdoor/adventure magazines, local media, and targeted events. Remember, word-of-mouth is powerful in this industry, so build a reputation for quality service and safe, unforgettable experiences.

4.6. Operations Plan

An operations plan provides a comprehensive overview of the logistics and day-to-day running of your business. This includes location, facilities, equipment, travel arrangements, safety provisions, staffing needs alongside their training and certifications. Your operations plan should detail strategies for managing the aforementioned whilst maintaining service quality and client satisfaction.

4.7. Risk Management Plan

Given the inherent risk associated with adventure tourism, a comprehensive risk management plan is essential. This should address risk identification, risk assessment, and appropriately tailored risk treatment strategies. Regular updating and reviewing of the risk management plan are necessary to keep pace with changing threat landscapes.

4.8. Partnerships and Collaborations

Finding opportunities for collaborations and partnerships can be a great way to expand your offerings, reach a wider audience, and mitigate risks. Build relationships with local communities, government bodies, international travel agencies, equipment providers, or other adventure tourism operators to explore the potential for fruitful partnerships.

4.9. Sustainable Practices

Promote and include sustainable practices in your business plan. Conscious travel is a rising trend amongst tourists, and your commitment to environmentally friendly practices will not only preserve your operating environment but also improve your business reputation and draw in a growing segment of eco-minded tourists.

4.10. Future Plans

As you grow, it is important to have plans for the future. These may include adding new experiences, associating with various facilitators, expanding to new locations, or any other ideas for growth and expansion. A well-outlined future plan shows potential for growth and can appeal to investors, partners, and consumers.

Remember, a business plan is not static - it evolves as your business grows and as the market changes. Regular revision and updating ensures you remain proactive and adaptable in this dynamic industry. Armed with an effective business plan, your adventure tourism business is one step closer to becoming a successful venture, appealing to the thrill-seekers and outdoor enthusiasts that make up your target market.

Chapter 5. Raising Your Banner: Branding and Marketing for Your Adventure Tourism Business

The first step to a successful adventure tourism business is developing a strong brand identity and marketing strategy. This critical first step will dictate how your potential customers perceive your business. Begin your venture by building a solid foundation and gradually, you'll see your brand's growth and evolution.

5.1. Identifying your Brand Identity

An often underappreciated aspect of any business is the development of its brand identity. This process involves creating a unique name, logo, and other symbolic elements that represent your organization. A brand identity serves as the blueprint of your business. It should clearly convey your company's mission, vision, and values to your target audience.

Use your adventure tourism's unique aspects to guide your branding decisions. Are you specializing in wilderness hikes, white-water rafting, or mountain climbing? No matter the adventure, your brand should clearly and creatively communicate this, allowing you to carve a distinct niche in the market.

Create a logo that is visually appealing and representative of your company's brand. Combine elements of adventure, thrill, and safety in the design so that it instantly resonates with the customer. Furthermore, adopt a color scheme and typography that aligns with your brand identity. Consistency across all branded materials can increase brand recall.

5.2. Building a Strong Web Presence

In today's digital age, having an online presence is a non-negotiable aspect of your business strategy. Websites serve as your business's digital storefront, where customers can access information about your services, make bookings, read reviews, and more, all at their convenience.

Your website should reflect your brand's identity and ethos. Be sure to include detailed and engaging descriptions of the experiences you offer. Images and videos of past adventures can increase engagement and demonstrate authenticity, while a blog section can provide value to your audience and boost Search Engine Optimization (SEO).

A strategic approach to SEO allows your website to rank higher on search engine results, making it easier to reach your target audience. Invest time and resources into learning about keywords relevant to your industry and incorporate them into your website content.

5.3. Utilization of Social Media Channels

One of the most powerful tools in your marketing arsenal is social media. Platforms like Instagram, Facebook, YouTube, and Twitter provide businesses unlimited opportunities to connect with their audience, promote their offerings, and even execute direct sales.

Create engaging and high-quality content that showcases your adventures. Videos, infographics, photos, live streams, customer testimonials, and behind-the-scenes footage are excellent ways to capture attention and convey your brand story.

Consider leveraging influencer partnerships. By collaborating with influencers whose followers align with your target audience, you can significantly broaden your reach and trust factor. Turning popular influencers into brand ambassadors can lead to a surge in bookings.

5.4. Email Marketing Tactics

Although some may believe that email marketing is outdated, it should not be overlooked. When done right, email marketing provides businesses with an exceptional return on investment. It's a highly effective way to distribute newsletters, updates, offers, and personalized messages.

Ensure you utilize a customer relationship management (CRM) system to manage, track, and analyze interactions and data throughout the customer lifecycle. It can help you retain customers, drive sales growth, and enrich your communication seamlessly.

5.5. Event Participation and Network Building

Your business exists within a broader system of adventure lovers, local guides, tourism agencies, and other relevant organizations. Participating in adventure tourism fairs, exhibitions, and similar events allows you to promote your brand, network with relevant parties, and gather insights on market trends.

5.6. Analyzing and Adapting

Brand and marketing strategies are never stagnant. They need constant analysis and adjustments based on evolving consumer behavior and market trends. Utilize Google Analytics or similar tools to identify successful strategies and those that need enhancements. Understand your customer feedback and always strive to exceed their expectations.

In essence, adventurous as it may sound, starting an adventure tourism business requires more than just a love for outdoor pursuits. A well-structured branding and marketing strategy is crucial. It defines your company's mission, carves your niche in a competitive market, builds customer relationships, and ultimately, determines the success of your venture. Happy adventuring, and successful strategizing!

Chapter 6. Trails to Revenue: Pricing Strategies and Revenue Streams

The journey from a mere inkling of a business idea to a tangible, successful venture is a trail filled with obstacles, but as every entrepreneur knows, the rewards are worth the struggle. Within the adventure tourism industry, this journey involves converting excitement and passion into viable revenue sources. And at the heart of this journey is a robust pricing strategy and understanding of potential revenue streams.

In pursuing sustainable profitability, crafting an effective pricing strategy for your adventure tourism services and diversifying your income streams is key. They determine not just your profitability, but also your business's longevity and scalability in the long term.

6.1. Understanding the Market and Competition

Adventure tourism is a competitive industry, which delivers unique experiences to its customers. As a result, understanding the market and competition is a fundamental first step in determining pricing. Carry out comprehensive market research and competitive analysis to uncover key market trends, demand patterns, and competitor pricing strategies.

Don't merely focus on businesses that appear similar to your proposed venture. Instead, be mindful of the broader tourism industry, seasonal trends, and changing consumer behaviour influenced by external factors such as economic changes or global events.

6.2. Pricing Models for Adventure Tourism

Many different pricing models can apply to adventure tourism businesses, depending on the nature and scale of the services provided. Here are a few commonly used ones:

1. Cost-Plus Pricing: This involves calculating the total cost per head (inclusive of all direct and indirect costs) and adding a specific margin to establish the price. Using this model is straightforward, but it may not always take into account the perceived value of the experience in the mind of the customer.

2. Competitive Pricing: Here, you would consider the prices charged by your competitors for similar experiences, then adjust your prices accordingly. But remember, making your service too cheap can make customers skeptical about its quality.

3. Value-Based Pricing: Based on this model, you would price your service based on the perceived or estimated value it adds to your customers' lives rather than just the service or experience itself. This can include factors like exclusivity, access to difficult-to-reach places, and expert guidance.

4. Dynamic Pricing: This model allows you to change prices based on demand, seasonality, and other market variables. Given the seasonality of some services in the adventure tourism industry, this can be an effective strategy.

Remember, when it comes to picking a pricing model, there's no one-size-fits-all strategy. The choice largely depends on your specific market and business conditions. Oftentimes, a hybrid model works best.

6.3. Setting Prices for Profitability

Once a fitting pricing model is chosen, the next stage involves setting the prices. Naturally, entrepreneurs want to profit from any business venture, but there are a few key considerations when deciding the price for adventure tourism services.

Firstly, you must cover all expenses—be they direct, indirect, fixed, or variable. Make sure your price covers the costs of every element involved in delivering the service. If you miss certain costs during this calculation, it could lead to underpricing, which can cut into your profit margins or even result in losses.

Incorporating a level of profitability in your pricing strategy is the next step. This can be a set figure per capita or a percentage markup across the board. Remember, this profit is what will drive your growth, so don't feel guilty about adding it in.

Lastly, remember that consumers in adventure tourism are looking for experiences and the price of these experiences often indicates quality or exclusivity. So, premium pricing can sometimes be a valid strategy too, if your offering justifies it.

6.4. Understanding and Incorporating Revenue Streams

While pricing forms the foundation of your revenue, it is the income diversification through multiple revenue streams that really fortifies it. Venture beyond the traditional ticket sales and consider these other revenue streams:

1. Merchandise: Branded hats, T-shirts, bags, or souvenir items related to the adventure experience can give customers a memento of their journey and boost your revenue.

2. Photography/Videography Services: Many adventurers love to have professional photographs or videos as souvenirs. You can offer these services at an additional fee.

3. Onsite Amenities: Food and beverage services, locker rentals, equipment rentals, or overnight accommodation if appropriate can generate substantial additional income.

4. Partnerships and Advertisements: Collaborating with other local businesses to promote their services can create a win-win situation. This could involve receiving a commission for each referral or having businesses advertise at your location or on your website.

5. Training and Certification: If your adventure activities require skill or understanding, providing courses and certifications can be an excellent revenue stream.

Remember, while diversifying revenue streams, ensure that they correspond to your brand image and customer expectations. Overdoing it can sometimes make your venture seem disingenuous.

6.5. Regularly Evaluate and Adjust

Finally, understand that pricing models and revenue streams will need revising over time. Regularly reviewing and adjusting your pricing and strategies based on market movements, competition, customer feedback, and business performance is key to continuous profitability.

Areas to consider while revising strategies can include the introduction of seasonal pricing, providing discounts or special packages for repeat or group customers, or offering value-add services based on consumer feedback.

In conclusion, navigating the trails to revenue in the adventure tourism industry may seem daunting, but with a solid understanding of your market and competition, an effective pricing strategy, diversified revenue streams, and regular evaluation and adjustments, the journey can be both profitable and rewarding.

Chapter 7. Risk and Reward: Understanding and Mitigating Liability

Engaging in outdoor adventure activities inherently includes elements of risk: the thrill of the quest, unpredictable weather, the vastness of the natural world. Consequently, as an adventure tourism business owner, understanding and effectively managing these risks is crucial to not only maintain a successful business but also ensure the safety and satisfaction of your clientele.

7.1. Understanding Liability in Adventure Tourism

Liability in the context of adventure tourism refers to the legal responsibility borne by your business for the safety and wellbeing of your customers during their participation in activities you offer. The key premise is the duty of care --- you, as a business, are obliged to reduce the potential risk of harm to a prudent minimum.

Factors that determine your business's liability include negligence, foreseeable harm, and breach of statutory duty. Consider negligence, a situation where the business fails to exhibit a standard of care reasonably expected. For instance, if you neglect regular equipment checks resulting in defective gear, the business could be deemed negligent. However, if an accident happens despite observance of meticulous safety checks and protocols, the concept of foreseeable harm is evaluated — could reasonable forethought have prevented the accident? Lastly, a breach of statutory duty refers to any infringement of laws or regulations associated with adventure tourism.

Understanding the intricacy of your business's liability helps shape effective measures to manage and mitigate liability risks.

7.2. The Essential Risk Assessment

A thorough risk assessment is instrumental in identifying and evaluating the possible hazards associated with each outdoor adventure activity you offer. For each identified risk, establish the probability and severity of occurrence. Additionally, recognize the section of your clientele that may be exceptionally susceptible to certain risks.

An effective risk assessment follows this general pattern:

1. Identify potential hazards.
2. Determine the likelihood of these risks.
3. Assess the severity of potential harm.
4. Identify vulnerable groups.
5. Develop protocols to mitigate identified risks.

Regularly review and update your risk assessment, recognizing that outdoor conditions and regulations change frequently.

7.3. Implementing Safety Standards and Procedures

Post risk assessment, you must incorporate effective safety standards and procedures. These include maintenance of equipment, safety training of staff, real-time monitoring of weather and environmental conditions, and pre-adventure briefings to clients. Ensure these procedures are comprehensive, clear, and adhered to by everyone involved in your adventure tourism operations.

Quality equipment, regularly inspected for potential wear and tear, significantly reduces risk exposure. Regular safety training for your team ensures they are up-to-date with safety protocols, emergency response processes, and first-aid treatments essential in decreasing severity in case of accidents.

Timely updates on weather and environmental conditions are pivotal. Extreme weather can necessitate the cancellation of activities. Lastly, ensure your clients understand the risks involved in the adventure activities and are briefed on safety measures to follow.

7.4. Insurance – An Indispensable Safety Net

Insurance serves as an indispensable safety net for your adventure tourism business. General liability, workers' compensation, and property insurance are necessary. Additionally, consider specialized adventure tourism insurance, covering specific risks unique to the industry.

While insurance is an added cost to your business, it provides much-needed protection and peace of mind in case of unforeseen incidents. Consequently, partnering with an insurance provider with robust knowledge of the outdoor adventure sector is advisable.

7.5. Legal Considerations and Waivers

To protect your business from legal claims or liabilities, consider having your clients sign a release of liability form or waiver. This document does not absolve you of all liabilities (especially in negligence cases), but it does help communicate the inherent risks associated with outdoor adventure activities.

However, waivers are subject to specific legal principles and differ from one jurisdiction to another; therefore, seeking legal counsel to draft a robust waiver is crucial.

7.6. Incident Management and Reporting

Even with the best risk mitigation strategies, incidents can occur. A robust Incident Management plan ensures effective response and communication during a crisis, while a structured Incident Reporting system records the incidence's details for future analysis and prevention strategies. Both play a significant role in displaying your commitment to safety and can help reduce liabilities.

Managing and mitigating liability in adventure tourism is multifaceted. However, with thorough understanding, thoughtful risk assessments, structured safety procedures, adequate insurance coverage, and legal protection, you can create an environment that prioritizes safety even in the midst of thrilling outdoor exploits. Thus, striking a balance between the exciting allure of adventure and prudent risk mitigation can provide longevity and profitability in the thrilling world of adventure tourism.

Chapter 8. Building Your Squad: Hiring and Training Outdoor Staff

The outdoor tourism business thrives on the skills and competencies of its staff. Therefore, a crucial part of starting your adventure tourism business is assembling your team. The more skilled, experienced, and adaptable the individuals you hire, the more successful your business will be. This chapter looks deeply into the hiring and training of your outdoor staff, from identifying potential candidates, to training, motivation, and retention strategies.

8.1. Identifying Your Team

The adventure tourism business isn't necessarily about hiring the most experienced outdoor enthusiasts. While experience is beneficial, it's more about finding individuals who are adaptable, quick to learn, and passionate about outdoor activities.

Look for individuals who have: + Personal passion for adventure & outdoors + Good communication and interpersonal skills + Previous experience in similar roles + Certifications in things like first aid, lifeguard certification, or other outdoor-specific qualifications + A demonstrable commitment to health and safety + Proof of physical fitness, mental resilience, and adaptability

To ensure that you're hiring staff who are best suited for your venture, formulate a strict recruitment process. This process should involve clearly defined job descriptions, an effective advertisement strategy, a rigorous interview process, and a thorough background check.

8.2. The Recruitment Process: Job Descriptions

A well-written job description clarifies the skills, qualifications, and traits you're looking for in your outdoor staff. It describes the role, responsibilities, and expectations, helping potential applicants understand what is required from them.

Ensure that the job description covers the following elements: + A clear, concise job title + A brief summary of the role + Detailed list of duties and responsibilities + The skills and qualifications required + Physical demands of the job + What the job offers in terms of compensation, personal development, and career progression.

8.3. Advertisement Strategy

The key to attracting the right candidates is strategic advertisement. Use both online and offline mediums, from job boards and social networks to local print media. Your advertisement should present a clear picture of your company's culture, mission, and unique offerings.

In your ads, emphasize your commitment to safety, environment preservation, and customer satisfaction. Include points that make your company appear attractive, such as the chance to work in spectacular outdoor settings, career advancement opportunities, and a supportive work environment.

8.4. Interview Process

Interview sessions serve as a great opportunity to gauge the suitability of prospective candidates beyond their resumes. This is your chance to check their interpersonal skills, their capability to thrive in a team, and their potential to create memorable experiences for your clients.

During the interview, ask open-ended questions related to adventure tourism, risk management, customer service, and teamwork. Make sure to check whether their values align with your company's ethos. Their responses should demonstrate reliability, inquisitiveness, adaptability, and a deep appreciation for the outdoors.

8.5. Background Checks

Never skip this step. A proper background check can help you avoid potential legal problems and ensure the safety of your clients. This includes checking references, criminal history, and any relevant certifications or credentials.

8.6. Training Your Staff

Once you've hired a capable team, the next step is to provide them with the necessary training. Training should focus on two key areas: skills development and knowledge creation.

Skills development involves honing their practical skills. These could range from navigation techniques to understanding local weather patterns, using survival equipment, managing wildlife encounters, and providing first aid. Regular drills should be carried out to ensure these skills remain sharp.

Knowledge creation involves educating your team about your business ethos, systems, guidelines, and safety protocols. Make sure they understand the importance of customer satisfaction and are equipped to uphold your company's standard of service.

8.7. Health and Safety

In adventure tourism, safety is paramount. Your staff needs to be fully aware of, and trained in, safety regulations and protocols. This includes regular risk assessment trainings, emergency response drills, and consistent emphasis on safety during their regular duties.

8.8. Motivating and Retaining Your Staff

Hiring is only part of the process; retaining your staff is another crucial aspect. Factors such as competitive pay, personal development opportunities, a work-life balance, a supportive management style, and a positive work environment all contribute to staff retention.

In adventure tourism, where the work can be physically demanding and comes with certain risks, showing that you deeply care about your staff's well-being leads to loyalty and commitment.

Finally, remember that feedback is vital. An open communication channel where your team can express their views, suggestions, and concerns fosters trust. Regular performance evaluations and recognition of hard work also add to the motivation levels of your staff.

In conclusion, the success of your adventure tourism business relies heavily on the team you build. This involves not just hiring the right people, but training them effectively, cementing a safety-first culture, and ensuring their motivation and satisfaction. This, in turn, will result in happy customers excited to return for more adventures with your company.

Chapter 9. Investment Outlay: Essential Equipment and Facilities

Setting up any business requires an initial investment for necessary equipment and facilities. In the adventure tourism business, this investment can vary widely depending on the nature and scale of activities you plan to offer. This chapter will walk you through the major areas where you will need to invest and provide an analysis of the potential costs involved.

9.1. Identification of Necessary Equipment

Before delving into the cost analysis, it is important to understand the range of equipment necessary to run an adventure tourism business. The type of activities you choose to offer would influence your equipment needs. For instance, gear required for rock climbing would differ vastly from those needed for scuba diving or mountain biking. Here are some common equipment categories across various adventure activities:

- Safety equipment: helmets, harnesses, ropes, carabiners, and climbing gears.

- Equipment specific to the activity: bikes, kayaks, skis, camping supplies, and so on.

- Navigation tools: GPS, compass, maps.

- First-aid supplies: emergency medical kits and rescue gear for any mishaps during the adventure.

- Special clothing: wetsuits, jackets, boots, gloves depending on the activity.

- Information Technology Infrastructure: computer systems, software for bookings and customer management, website creation and maintenance.

Remember equipment will need to be replaced periodically due to wear and tear. Thus, part of your annual budget should be allocated for maintenance and replacement of equipment.

9.2. Evaluation and Procurement

Once you have identified the necessary equipment, it's time to evaluate and procure them. Consider these steps:

- Research suppliers for quality and cost: Look for trusted brands and compare prices across suppliers. You might get discounts for bulk orders.

- Check for warranty and maintenance terms: Ensure the equipment comes with a warranty period and regular maintenance.

- Consider buying used equipment: If the budget is tight, check online marketplaces or liquidation sales to find used gear at a significantly lower price. Before buying, always verify the condition and safety of the equipment.

9.3. Setup of Facilities

The facility for an adventure tourism business is essentially its operating base. This may include an office for managing bookings and administrative work, storage for equipment, and perhaps a training area. You might also need permits to use natural sites for your activities. Here are some factors to consider:

- Location: The location should be convenient for tourists and near your activity sites. Rent or purchase costs can vary widely depending on the location.

- Size: The office should have enough space to store all your equipment, and comfortable working space for staff.

- Layout and design: If customers will visit your office, it needs to be inviting and professional. You might need to invest in design and furnishing.

- Utilities: Factor in the costs of electricity, water, and internet connections.

- Permits: If you are operating in a national park or protected area, check the rules and costs of permits/fees involved.

Don't forget to factor in ongoing costs such as rent/mortgage, maintenance, insurance, and utility bills.

9.4. Digital Infrastructure

In this digital era, your web presence is as important as the physical. It could be a major source of customer acquisition. Here's what to consider:

- Website setup: You'll need a user-friendly website that provides information about your activities, prices, booking options, and contact details.

- Booking System: Your website should include a secure online booking system.

- Social Media and SEO: Invest in social media and SEO to increase your online visibility.

- IT Equipment: Computer systems, printers, software for managing bookings, customer data, and accounting.

The investment in digital infrastructure can vary based on the level of sophistication and your technical skills. You might need professional help for setup and maintenance, especially for SEO and online marketing.

9.5. Manpower and Training

You'll need staff: guides who have expertise in the adventure activities, administrative staff for bookings, and possibly an IT professional for maintaining the website and online presence. You would also want to invest in their training and certification where required.

9.6. Marketing and Promotion

Marketing requires a budget. Initially, you might want to advertise locally or across popular tourist hubs. Online marketing on social networks has become a cost-effective way to reach a global audience. Participating in travel trade fairs, advertising on travel websites, and so on, can help you reach your target customers.

9.7. Insurance

It is crucial to have adequate insurance coverage considering the inherent risks involved in adventure activities. You will need insurance for liability and protection of your assets like equipment. The cost for insurance can vary depending on the risk level of the activities you offer.

To summarize, the investment outlay for an adventure tourism business can be considerable and involves a range of equipment, digital and physical infrastructures, manpower, marketing, and insurance. Thorough planning, research, and smart procurement can help optimize the costs. It is best to start with a well-researched business plan that outlines your services, identifies necessary investments, and projects the potential profitability.

Chapter 10. Selling the Experience: Crafting Exciting Itineraries

Fundamentally, crafting exciting itineraries is all about storytelling. It's your chance to orchestrate an unforgettable series of journeys and experiences that will not only entice your customers, but stay with them long after they've returned home. Just like telling a captivating story, creating an engaging itinerary requires a deep understanding of your audience, a compelling narrative, and the elements of surprise and delight.

10.1. Getting to Know Your Audience

Engaging with your potential customers and understanding their interests, preferences, and expectations are the key initial steps. Some customers may be thrill-seekers, aiming to conquer wild terrains and fierce rivers, while others may wish for a more relaxed immersion into the pristine beauty of nature. The ability to identify, anticipate and cater to this disparate range of desires is an invaluable skill.

Conduct in-depth market research through means such as surveys, feedback forms, online forums, or direct interviews to understand your target customers' preferences. Demographic analysis—considering the age, physical ability, economic background, and cultural influences of your prospective audience—is also essential.

Analyze the competition. An understanding of what your competitors offer can be insightful, but always remember to maintain your unique selling proposition. Using this data, you can accurately cater your adventure tourism business to the needs and preferences of your chosen audience.

10.2. Building A Compelling Narrative

Once you've understood your audience, the next step is to craft a compelling narrative around your adventure offerings—this is the story you want the customers to live and remember. Each trip is a distinct narrative, and every destination is a new chapter. In between, there are numerous opportunities to create unforgettable moments and experiences.

The inclusion of local culture, for instance, adds an enriching layer to the experience. Introducing your guests to indigenous communities, letting them partake in traditional practices, or tasting local cuisines can foster deep connections between them and the places they visit. Every destination has its unique history and tales, and including these into your itineraries can make the trip feel special and personalized.

10.3. From Structure to Flexibility: Balancing the Itinerary

A well-structured itinerary acts as a blueprint for your tour. It outlines where travelers will go, what they will do, and how they will achieve their desired experiences. However, it must also allow flexibility to adapt to unexpected circumstances, such as changes in weather or clients' whims.

All structured activities should be thoroughly planned and organized, with time and resources accounted for. Safety should always be a priority in this structure - for instance, ensuring participants are well-equipped and properly briefed for adventure sports.

Striking a balance between organized activities and free time is critical. Free time not only gives a client the opportunity to explore on their own but also makes room for rest and personal reflection.

10.4. Infusing Elements of Surprise and Delight

Unexpected, thoughtful touches, such as a surprise gourmet picnic arranged at a heavenly vista, gifts showcasing local craftsmanship, or a meet-and-greet with a local wildlife expert, can make a trip truly memorable.

These elements of surprise don't always need to be extravagant, they can range from an unexpected stop at a scenic viewpoint to a friendly chat with local fishermen. The key lies in personal touches that signify you care about your guests and enrich their experience.

10.5. Creating Emotional Connections

Remember, you're selling more than just a service; you're selling an experience. If you can tap into the emotional needs of your clientele and tailor those experiences accordingly, your tours will become something more than just a product – they'll become memories that your customers cherish. This emotional bond with your brand can drive repeated business and valuable word-of-mouth referrals.

Keeping this in mind while designing and executing your itineraries greatly enhances the client's overall experience. Whether it's the adrenaline rush of white-water rafting, the serene joy of watching a mountain sunset, or the awe of a cultural revelation, these moments knit themselves into the emotional fabric of your guests, invariably making their journey with you extraordinary and unforgettable.

10.6. Review & Refinement: Towards A Dynamic Itinerary

Finally, just as every journey makes a traveler richer, every tour should make your itineraries richer too. The process of itinerary design doesn't end after crafting it. It's a dynamic process that you will constantly need to refine and adjust based on travelers' feedback, changes in local settings, or the arrival of new experiences that might elevate your offerings.

Keep engaging with your customers post-trip, understand what they appreciate most, what could be improved, or what was missing. This continuous feedback loop will keep your adventure tourism business fresh and relevant, ensuring a constant evolution towards perfection.

And remember, an itinerary is not merely an arrangement of places, activities, and experiences. It's a symphony, a story, a journey. It's the anticipation of an adventure and the satisfaction of an experience well-lived. Craft your itineraries with care, and watch as your business thrives, one memorable trip at a time.

Chapter 11. Forward March: Scalability and Growth Strategies

In the thrilling journey of operating an adventure tourism business, scalability and adopting effective growth strategies is as impactful as choosing the right equipment for a difficult expedition. Your business's ability to grow without collapsing under its own weight is an art in itself, requiring thoughtful planning and execution.

11.1. Understanding Scalability

Scalability refers to your business's ability to handle increased workload without compromising performance or outputs. It is the capacity to expand production efficiently when resource usage is scaled up. So, why does this matter for adventure tourism companies?

This industry is highly competitive and is likely to experience ebbing and flowing demand according to seasonality or other external forces. How efficiently you manage to serve a growing number of clients, without sacrificing the quality of their experience, determines the success and growth of your business.

→ Understand your current capacity: begin by evaluating your ability to manage the current demand, ensuring that every client receives satisfactory service.

→ Assess the potential for growth: look at the market trends and demographics, your competition, and factor in your company's unique offerings to estimate potential growth.

→ Develop a scalable business model: this should be flexible, fashioning a roadmap for managing an increased volume of clients and offering a variety of services.

11.2. Financial Strategies for Scalability

Implementing successful financial strategies is a critical part of achieving scalability. A growing venture will encounter a wave of financial challenges.

→ Cash flow management: liquidity is paramount to handle growth. Round up reserves for emergencies, and manage receivables, payables, and inventory efficiently.

→ External financing: you might need extra financial resources for growth. Consider loans, grants, partnerships, or investors, but ensure each move aligns with your long-term goals.

→ Profit & loss (P&L) management: a detailed understanding of your business expenses and income sources can assist in forecasting profits and determining viable growth paths.

11.3. Operational Strategies for Scalability

Strategic operations management ensures that your business can handle the challenges of growth. Seek procedures and systems that enhance efficiency without compromising on your clients' experience.

→ Process optimization: streamline processes with a focus on minimising waste and maximising efficiency to handle larger operations with ease.

→ Quality Assurance: despite the rush of scaling-up, never compromise on the quality of your services. Establish a set quality standard and stick to it consistently.

→ Outsourcing: Some tasks may not be critical for your in-house team to handle. Explore outsourcing options for such tasks to ensure cost-effectiveness.

11.4. Marketing and Sales Strategies for Scalability

Growth strategies demand amplified marketing efforts and robust sales techniques to drive business forward.

→ Diversification of services: Venture into untapped market segments by providing a variety of experiences that cater to a diverse clientele.

→ Marketing strategies: craft a marketing plan focusing on brand positioning, pricing strategies, and communication channels that cater to your target audience's preferences.

→ Partnership opportunities: analyze the potential benefits of partnerships – they can pave the way for shared resources, expertise, and expanded market reach.

11.5. Leveraging Technology for Scalability

In our tech-savvy world, leveraging technology is not an option, it's a requirement.

→ CRM solutions: appraising customer relationship management (CRM) software can enable an organized approach to managing your rapidly growing client base.

→ Online booking platforms: for easier booking management and to reach a wider audience, consider the use of online booking platforms.

→ Automation: technology can also assist with automating repetitive and administrative tasks, freeing up your team to focus on service delivery.

In essence, growing your adventure tourism business demands conscious consideration for scalability, astute financial planning, and adept operational and marketing strategies. It's your journey towards crafting memorable experiences on a larger scale, rich with challenges and opportunities. Your success depends on combining passion with business acumen, and the courage to tread uncharted territories. Latch on to this adventure; it's awaiting your command.

www.ingramcontent.com/pod-product-compliance
Lightning Source LLC
Chambersburg PA
CBHW062304290526
45794CB00006B/2696

9798856607849